The Busy Woman's Guide to Faith

Moving Beyond Busy To Affirm
The Life God Created For You

Tamika S. Washington

The Busy Woman's Guide to Faith : Moving Beyond Busy To Affirm The Life God Created For You

Copyright © 2020 by Tamika S. Washington.

All rights reserved. Printed in the United States of America. No part of this book may be used or reproduced in any manner whatsoever without written permission except in the case of brief quotations embodied in critical articles or reviews.

Published by :
Relentless Publishing House, LLC

www.relentlesspublishing.com

ISBN: 978-1-948829-52-6

First Edition: April 2020

10 9 8 7 6 5 4 3 2 1

Dedication

To God's gift to me, my husband, Devin & my amazing darling little Faith Bellamy.

My grandma Sarah & my momma who believes in me and knows the path God has set before me.

My mother in law Rosetta who has cheered my writing on from the sidelines since 2018.

My sister in law and aunts who live, move, and exemplifies the essence of women of faith.

My faithful tribe of friends-too many to name but you know who you are. I love my sistas.

TABLE OF CONTENTS

Foreword 2

We Must Get Unbusy 5

Affirmation One 9

Affirmation Two 19

Affirmation Three 27

Affirmation Four 33

Affirmation Five 39

Affirmation Six 47

Affirmation Seven 53

Affirmation Eight 59

About the Author 69

Foreword

I will never forget the day I walked in Converspace to meet the owner, Tamika Shuler Washington. It was an instant connection and I knew she was a woman of faith. Over time, I learned that she has a toddler daughter like me, was newly married and wore many other hats. I could relate to Tamika's life on almost every level. Life was busy all the time! One thing I learned quickly is how to integrate my family in my busy work life. A business trip to the beach would look like a family vacation all in one trip. My husband driving me while my toddler assistant played with her device turned my name into a song and talked to me during the drive as if she was a teenager. Before the integration of family and just taking a pause, I was stressed out a lot, frustrated and even got depressed a few times because I would do the work of God but stop seeking the God of the work. I would be busy but not productive. Tamika talks about how being busy is not good and not continuing to yield to God can lead to danger and her turning point to do things different lead her to write this powerful book to help more women of faith get unbusy in order to grow.

Tamika is the best person to write this book because not only have I seen Tamika grow in her faith but her ability to say,

"No," with a straight face and give herself grace. I have learned so much in this season from Tamika Shuler Washington but the major things that sticks with me daily is to give myself grace, surrender daily through prayer and tune into God.

Joy McLaughlin-Harris
Touch of Joy International, LLC

The Busy Woman's Guide to Faith

Why We Must Get Unbusy

When I first started my business, I knew that opening doors for the first time to the public would require a lot of time from me. I knew I would impact people and grow in exponential ways. What I didn't know was that business would take up a lot of my time, and I wasn't ready or prepared to sacrifice my time. In my head, I pictured working my 9-5 and coming home to spend time with my family. I pictured vacation-filled spring breaks and days of kicking my feet up and basking in the moments of treasured time. I imagined all of this. I experienced none of this. While I was built for the job, I wasn't prepared for it.

There is a quote that says, "Proper planning prevents poor performance, (P5 Rule)." A huge part missing from the equation was how I spent my time PREPARING.

Time is so important and we often take it for granted, sometimes not remembering that we can't get it back. Never! As Christ-living beings, we must be conscious of how we spend our time. What was missing for me was I didn't spend enough time preparing with My Lord. I found myself on a whirlwind tornado path of doing EVERYTHING.

Days would go without devotion, prayer or giving thanks. I adopted the busy woman complex. It bled through my attitude and my tears after no one signed up for business.

As a blogger, I wrote so much about the busy woman and here I was warping into that person. God's Word tells us, "*Be very careful, then, how you live – not as unwise but as wise, making the most of every opportunity, because the days are evil."* (Ephesians 5:15-16).

Let's be honest, being busy is not of God. It's not productive. It's not wise.

Acknowledge this with me please-society has created this super busy super woman in us. It has become the norm. We put on the capes daily. Trying to do it all and be all, when in all actuality, we are nothing. I don't mean that in a negative way, but even the Word tells us that we are filthy rags (Isaiah 64:6). A part of changing is acknowledging and confessing.

Ladies, confess with me:
Lord forgive me for trying to be super and busy with everything. I surrender my super womanness over to you for You alone are the only super being in my life.

A part of spending our time wisely is that we as women have to surrender daily through prayer, meditating, tuning in to God and affirming our Christ walk. By doing this, we hear from God. The Bible tells us that the steps of a good man are ordered by the Lord (Psalm 27:23). Therefore, when we allow God to order our steps and direct our paths, we know how to better spend our time. When we spend our time with God, we get strategies to prepare for the enemy's attack. When we prepare for the trials that come our way, we have more peace.

The P5 Rule (Proper Preparation Prevents Poor Performance) has a Biblical connection y'all. Ladies, when we properly prepare with the Word, we avoid poor performance. I'm not trying to sound deep here, but what I am saying is preparation is about our time and how we spend our time wisely.

God says, "I have the right to do anything, you say – but not everything is beneficial. I have the right to do anything" – but not everything is constructive." (1 Corinthians 10:23). However, everything is not bad and we don't have to do everything. What we should be prepared to do in order to be the best at what we do, is seek first the Kingdom of God and all His right ways.

I understand there are busy seasons in life preparing for school, pregnancy, weddings and new jobs. If we equip ourselves, those busy seasons will not take us off track, but instead bring us closer to God.

Affirmation One:
I will wait with expectations (Stop wanting it so bad)

Isaiah 40:31

I remember working for America's #1 wireless company at a local store in Buford, Georgia. It was a Sunday afternoon, hours before a big Atlanta Falcons game. The store was filled with blaring sounds of ESPN, registers chiming from countless sales and in walks one angry customer who changed the entire atmosphere. He was red. His blood was boiling. He proceeded to shout at me the problem he was experiencing with his device. I paused to look up his account, as we did with every customer.

I went through the motions of apologizing, reassuring, and going through his account history- all the protocols we were trained to take. Before I went to offer to have his phone looked at, I asked him to do one thing,"Will you wait for just a second while I check with the technician for some options to assist you?" He grumbled under his breath while I stepped away. I knew he was eager to join the Falcons festivities because he was donned in a t-shirt, checked out the pre-game chat on ESPN and repeatedly looked at his watch.

After waiting five minutes, I received some great news. We would update his phone without extending his contract because of some manufacturer issues with his current phone. In the midst of getting the new phone set up, the customer became very impatient and slammed his current phone against the counter while yelling angrily at me. The old phone was now cracked, which was not covered under warranty and could not be shipped back to the manufacturer in the current cracked condition. He ruined his chance to get a new phone all because he did not have the patience to wait.

How many times do we do less waiting and more taking matters into our own hands? We all can relate to the angry customer. We sometimes lack patience, focus and understanding. We jump into relationships, jobs, positions and new business ventures because sometimes we lack the patience to simply wait. Waiting is difficult if we are honest with ourselves. It is a difficult process for two reasons: we don't know the outcome and society has made us believe that we can have anything anytime we want.

Ladies, confess with me:
Because we all are guilty of leaning on our own understanding, we ask that you forgive us Lord. We will put our trust in you.

How often do we rush God or try to pressure Him to answer us right away? I can honestly admit and raise both of my hands indicating yep, that's been me before. There is a reason we have to wait. During this season of waiting, God is asking us to do more. First, God is **building up our faith** in Him. If we immediately received the blessing He had in store for us, we would not appreciate it as much.

A part of building up our faith includes God pruning us. John 15:2 tells us that Jesus prunes any branch that does not bear fruit. God wants us to be prepared to receive what He has in store for us. If we are carrying dead weight, we can't be strengthened holding onto things, people and situations that are holding us back.

Let us be reminded of King David. He did not become a king immediately. In fact, it wasn't until later in his life around 30 that he obtained his crown. Before David became king, under Saul's leadership, he was threatened by Saul and Saul attempted to kill David several times. Through all of the turmoil with his leader Saul, David's faith was building up. God protected him along the way, strengthened his skills and provided resources for him to defeat on the battlefield.

David was far from perfect as we all are far from perfect, but his faith in God and his loyalty to God deemed him the leader he was called to be. Hebrews 11 reminds us that without faith it is impossible to please God. As we go through this season of waiting, we must let God build and strengthen our faith.

As we wait, God is **guiding us on the right path**. The Bible says that the steps of a good man are ordered by God. In order for God to guide our steps, we have to put ourselves aside and follow Him. Can I be honest? That's not easy. We deal with our flesh every day, but we MUST lay aside every weight, fear, unforgiveness, control and habits. Not doing so causes us to NOT hear the Shepherd's voice.

Carrying these weights only causes a riff in our relationship with God and causes us to be distracted. When we are distracted, we are not tuning in to our Father, which means we are not being guided by Him. When God is guiding us, He is *protecting* us and making *provisions* for us.

One of God's many promises is to protect us. In Isaiah 54:17 we are reminded that, "No weapon formed against us shall prosper…" When we think about Moses and the children of Israel, we remember that God protected Israel from Pharaoh and the Egyptians when He slowed them down in the Red Sea, destroying their chariots and drowning them in the water.

Now the children of Israel were something y'all. I know God was like, 'Here they go again with all that complaining.' In the wilderness, that's what was happening. The Israelites were complaining and saying that it was better to go back to Egypt where they would be able to eat and get fattened. Really Israelites? What did God do for them? He provided some finger-licking good ole manna.

I imagine their faces as they were eating the manna just over-indulging in it as if it was a delicious piece of red velvet cake covered in cream cheese icing and sprinkled with pecans. Yummm! Manna was everywhere, falling from the sky. This showed God's supernatural power and provisions to sustain His children He loved so dearly. Think about your own life. How many times were you quenching something or longing for a blessing and God just made it rain down from Heaven? Right now, let us take the time to thank Him for protecting us and providing for us.

Through His protection and provisions, we know for SURE that God is guiding us and for all He's done and more, He gets the glory!

Finally, during this season of waiting, we **become totally dependent on God**. Let us go back to Moses. God told Moses that He was going to send him back into Egypt to confront Pharaoh, a ruler who groomed and respected Moses. Now Moses was humble in all his ways, but even that was not going to help him. God instructed Moses that he was going to have to put aside all of his ways and totally depend on Him.

Every day Americans depend on their bank accounts, their families, their 401Ks and their connections. We love to say, "It's not what you know, but who you know." Well let me share the lesson God showed me about 'who you know.' I believe with all my heart that God ordains and orders our steps. That's what the word says. God will definitely position us to meet the right people and be in the right places at the right time. I put myself in a position to depend on someone to grow my business and connect me with all the right people. I was so blinded by their "success" that I was not tuned in and God definitely wasn't guiding me.

You can know many great people, but if the connections are not ordained by God, it does not matter. Through that situation, I lost time, faith and money but God used that situation to remind me that the only person I need to know is Him. In this life, you'll meet a lot of great people who can do a lot of amazing things, but if connecting with them is not through God say, "Hi, bless you and keep it moving." You never want to put yourself in a situation where you depend on someone else's connections to get you in all the right places. If it's meant to be, it will happen, but only when you are being guided by God and when you are totally dependent on Him.

Many times in our lives we are going to have to wait, but know that God is providing for us, protecting and positioning us for the promises that are to come because of our faithfulness in waiting. Let us not forget how God positions us because positioning us is a part of the expectation. However, if we are doing our own thing, being misguided and depending on other things or people, we'll miss the hand of God working behind the scenes. You may be struggling financially or dealing with a difficult relationship, but your lack of patience and dim outlook on life will not allow you to trust God. He is always, ALWAYS, working things out on our behalf.

When my daughter started walking, I had to clear the path, lay around some pillows and soft toys as a barrier between her and the floor. My husband and I would practice with her by putting her in between our stretched out legs so that if she fell she would fall on our legs and not the bare floor, or we would stretch our arms out to let her feel safe as she practiced walking. She never cried because she couldn't get it right. She just laughed and tried again. God does the same for us. He puts barriers around us to protect us. He clears paths for us as He guides us. He whispers soft reminders in our ears to tell us to keep going. The Word of God tells us that He is a lamp to our feet, a light on our path (Psalm 119:105). He is setting us up and positioning us for the blessing that's to come.

Will you trust Him totally while you wait with expectation? Don't smash the phone like my angry customer. Don't grumble like the Children of Israel. Just wait with expectation knowing that God provides, protects, and positions us for His promises.

Is there anything you are waiting for God to fulfill in your life? Of course you are waiting on His promises, but this is a time for you to be specific in your prayers. Date this page and list out what you are waiting for God to fulfill. While you are waiting, what areas do you need Him to work out in you? This is your time to TOTALLY show God you are depending on Him. Take it a step further and find scriptures that align with your specific areas of prayers. Come back and cross your answered prayers and areas of growth off the list as He fulfills these areas in your life. "But *they that wait* upon the *LORD* shall renew their strength" (Isaiah 40:31).

Prayer: Lord, You are a Promise keeper. You give us everything we need in Your Perfect timing. We confess to you right now that there are times we could not wait. We acknowledge our short falls of patience, lack of trust in your outcome, and our failure to simply wait. You are the one true source of Help.

Based on what you read, what truths or promises from God will you affirm over your life? Write your affirmation in the box below.

Affirmation Two: I can make wise decisions
(I don't know everything)

Proverbs 3:13

I remember my fifth year of teaching. My principal moved me to a new grade level with a different set of teachers and a brand new group of students. During this particular school year, I was given the task of a leadership position, coaching a cheer team and starting a new passion for managing social media accounts. As the school year went on, I added little things to my plate. Yes, I'll teach your after school class for you. Yes, I'll look into a vendor opportunity for you. Sure, I'll post to your account every day instead of three days a week. Good idea-let's start that entrepreneur group. Before I knew it, I was saying a lot of yes's. I was bursting out of the seams. My plate was overflowing. My life was full.

I had many seasons of saying yes in my life. I remember telling God that I was tired of people depending on me. Call Tamika. She's great at writing papers. Call Tamika. She'll tell you how to handle your education issue. Now don't get me wrong, I enjoy lending a hand, skill and ear when people asked, but over the years, I've learned there are God-assignments that we miss because we are so busy saying yes to people-assignments.

Do you remember the story of Martha and Mary when Jesus came to visit? Martha was so distracted with household and serving duties, that she failed to see that none of those things were important as a visit from Jesus. Can you imagine Jesus showing up at your house. "Yes Jesus. Come on in. Have a seat right there and don't come in the kitchen while I'm cooking and cleaning."

There is nothing wrong with serving. In fact, Martha was gearing up to serve a meal to Jesus, but that wasn't important. What I love about the story as well is Jesus listened to her concerns just as He hears ours. However, she missed the God-assignment at that moment to sit with Jesus and learn of the bread of life through Him.

Sometimes our life is so busy we can't see some important things that God has in store for us. Sometimes our life is so busy we even neglect the One who is most important to us. Sometimes our lives are so busy we make unwise choices.

Here is a lesson for many of us. The reason we are taking on too much is because we are not being wise in our decision-making processes with our lives. **Ladies, you are** important. **You are more than enough. Stop letting people make you feel otherwise.** We'll discuss this more in the next affirmation. Before I dig deeper about why I'm stressing this, let's talk about wisdom and why we have to be wise in the decisions we make DAILY!

Ladies, confess with me:
I have not been wise in my decisions so help me to put my faith in you as I make decisions daily. You are the author and finisher of my faith.

Much of what we decide comes from knowledge and experience. When it comes to making decisions, we have to be wise. Wisdom is defined as "the quality of having experience, knowledge and good judgement," (dictionary.com). We can all admit that there are times when we don't use our best judgement.

I remember I paid my car off, was six months in my new house and was making pretty good money as an educator. In previous years, I helped with the after school program and was told that I would be over the program in the upcoming school year. In my mind, I calculated extra money means. I can go buy the car I've been eyeing for a few months now and I did just that. I bought a new car. Lo and behold, new administration came in the building and decided to use the old program coordinator, and that meant no extra money for me. Needless to say, I struggled a few months after buying the car. I knew that was not a wise decision. I was quick to satisfy my wants at the time and not my needs.

What does this all mean you may be asking? Sometimes we get caught up in situations because we lack wisdom in saying no, not right now. When we give in to our wants, our fleshly desires, or to others, we leave no room for what really should be taking place in our lives. Maybe like me, you made a bad financial decision or maybe you've taken on too many tasks and you're overwhelmed. It happens to us all.

Let's think about what would happen if we were wise in our decision-making. The Bible tells us in Psalm 111:10, "The *fear of the Lord is the beginning of wisdom*." The fear here is not talking about being afraid or scared, but it is about *reverence and honoring God*. When we reverence and honor Him, we know that we cannot do anything without Him. That means we cannot and should not make decisions without Him. We've tried many times in our life to do things on our own, without seeking God and end up crawling right back to Him for direction. Hello! That's why Proverbs tells us to, *"Trust in the Lord with ALL of our hearts and do not lean on your understanding."* Doing things your way? Tell me how that's working out for you. In my car situation, it didn't work out too well.

So how should we go about getting wisdom and getting better at making wise decisions? First things first, honor and reverence God at all times. Acknowledge Him in everything.

1. **Read God's Word**. Make it a habit to dive in the Word consistently. The Bible tells us in Joshua 1:8, "This book of the law shall not depart out of your mouth; but you shall meditate therein day and night, that you may observe to do according to all that is written therein…" Sometimes we are so busy doing other things or managing our daily lives, that our study time is not a priority. Let's all do better and make it a priority this week.

2. **Apply God's Word**. We are called to be doers of the Word and not just hearers of the Word. When the Word of God tells us how to forgive, let's give it a shot. Forgiveness is huge in our faith walk. When the Word shows us how to increase our faith, let's give it a shot. Faith is important in our daily journey. Where the Word tells us to show love,

let's do that. Loving others can be hard at times, but your love for someone could be the very thing that leads them to Christ.

3. ***Look to God.*** The scriptures give us direct insight on Christ and how to live. When we don't have an answer, ask God for wisdom and understanding. God's Word promises to give us what we need. He says "...you will call upon me and come and pray to me, and I will hear you. You will seek me and find me, when you seek me with all your heart. I will be found by you, declares the Lord..." Jeremiah 29:12-14.

4. ***Cry out to God.*** Pray out loud to God and ask Him for what you need. Ask Him for instruction, insight and guidance. When you ask, believe with your whole heart that He will answer your prayer. *"Call unto me, and I will answer thee, and show thee great and mighty things which thou knowest not,"* (Jeremiah 33:3).

In life, we have choices. In my teaching career, I chose to take on too many tasks, which led to an overwhelmed body and underdeveloped soul. We can choose to honor God daily, even in our decisions. Even when I purchased my car, tuning in to God would have let me know that it was not the right time for a big purchase. For every situation we face, there is an answer. The right answer happens when we make wise decisions.

Think about a time when you didn't make a wise choice. What was the outcome? What would you do differently? Understand this is not a negative reflection and if we want to change our behaviors, we must understand the choices we make so that we can avoid the same patterns in the future

Prayer: Father you are an all-knowing, all-wise God. I can do all things through you so that you can be glorified. Help me to be wise in my decisions by seeking you first.

Based on what you read, what truths or promises from God will you affirm over your life? Write your affirmation in the box below.

Affirmation Three: I can say no confidently

(Stop taking on too much)

Proverbs 3:26

Let's be real ladies. There are only 24 hours in a day and 7 days a week. Where in the world do we have the room to squeeze in *just one more thing?* Here is the problem with us. Saying yes is easy, while saying no is simply too hard. For some odd reason, no seems to carry this negative connotation. In our minds *'no'* is a rejection; something bad. The problem is when we don't say *'no'*, we are adding more to our lives than we should. I read a blog post about this same topic and it said, "*Saying yes to everything means you have no time for anything.*" You can't possibly go to every event when you're invited. You can't have coffee every time your friend calls. You can't volunteer for every service project. You can't bake the cookies for every school bake sale. You can't lead every group study. You are one person. You can't do it all.

Ladies, confess with me:

"Saying yes all the time won't make me Wonder Woman. It will make me a worn out woman[1]"

[1] The Best Yes by Lysia Turkyest Chapter 12: The Awkward Disappointment of Saying No from The Best Yes

What does no really mean in our lives? Oftentimes we pray for something. We want God to give us the green light to 'go'. We want to hear a yes from Him. However, we get a 'No'. Not for you. Not your time. Not right now. Days, weeks, or months go by and we begin to understand His 'No'. It was for our own good. The bible tells us that King David in his latter years after establishing his wealthy kingdom wanted to build the temple. He inquired of God and was told no. God had another person in mind to build the temple and it was David's son, Solomon. Instead, David helped fulfill God's purpose by providing all the material that was needed to build the temple. David was a man of war but think about the temple of God. It's the holiest of holy, a place of peace. Even God gives us a **powerful no** so that He can give us His most powerful yes. And guess what? He wants you to learn the powerful No. Remember the previous affirmation was about wisdom. I hope you were encouraged to know that every decision you make, you should include God in your decision-making. See the connection here.

When we are wise in our decision-making, we get to give our best yes to God!

The reason you need to say no to the PTA bake sale is because it is going to take up too much of your time organizing it and that time could have taken away from the task God was going to place on your to-do list. Or, maybe your child will need some extra TLC after feeling defeated from a ball game. Or, your husband finds out he is getting a promotion and wants to celebrate the good news so you need to be ready to celebrate your man. We never know how we may need to be in position for a best yes. For a task that would bring God glory and honor. We just never know what God has in store for us and if we are too busy, we can't make room for the best yes. Besides, you did the bake sale last year. Let someone else do that.

Wait a minute! "I've already said yes." We've all been there too.

"Sure I'll be happy to do that." "No worries. I'll get that done by tomorrow." I recently said that statement to someone and found myself regretting every word as they that rolled off my tongue.

Do you realize there were times that Jesus said no to the people? Jesus was on a journey, healing the sick, casting out demons and everyone was impressed by these miracles. He was gaining a lot of popularity. Jesus continues doing His thing with large crowds watching through the night.

In Mark 1:35-38 we learn that Jesus left early in the morning to pray away from the crowds. The disciples that were with

Him found Him alone. "Jesus, the people are waiting for you," they exclaimed. However, they were not expecting the answer Jesus gave them. He advised them to follow Him as He went to the next town to preach. Remember, Jesus came to be the Savior of the world. Not just a healer and to cast out demons. Not just to feed the hungry. His intention was always to preach the message and save the world not just in that one area where the healing took place. He said no so that He could answer His God-given assignment.

Here is the point:

1. Don't feel bad if you say no. I promise there are several people after you who will say yes.
2. Acknowledge God in your decision-making. He will never steer you wrong.
3. Save room on your schedule for you. There is nothing wrong with saying no so that you can unwind and relax.

Decide what is important to you and start prioritizing things in your life. Make room in your life to give God, your family and your ministry your yes!

Prayer: Lord help us in what we do to align our daily walk with Your will so that we can say yes to our God-given assignments at all times. Get rid of the need to please, the power to control and the feeling of being liked and replace it with your joy, strength, and perfect way.

Based on what you read, what truths or promises from God will you affirm over your life? Write your affirmation in the box below.

Affirmation Four: I will trust that God will work things out (Stop taking matters in my own hands)

Romans 8:28

We all love a good action-packed movie where some hero in a cape comes to save the day. I'm not much of a superhero comic girl but I love the Avengers. All of them. If you pay attention to the storyline, they are all the same-villan does something bad, the world is turned upside down, the hero jumps and saves the day. In any action-heroic film, you'll find the same.

For some reason an action-heroic character has crept into our lives as women and we've embraced the cape. Society has created superwomen, having us to believe that we can do anything, solve every problem, can go anywhere, be strong at all times, lead at all times and be everything to everyone.

There was a poster created after World War II of a woman rolling up her sleeves, wearing a bandana, and flexing her muscles. Her name was Rosie and we've been told countless stories about Rosie being a frontleader in the feminist movement and how she was a heroic icon for women. Here is the reality. Rosie was a regular woman and the poster was not as popular as we believe (History.com, March 2020). If you research Naomi Parker Fraley, you'll find the truth.

Here's a truth that is more important. What society has us believing about ourselves is a myth. In reality, we are not superwomen. We are human and as humans, God created us with a range of emotions and abilities to fulfill His will so that He may be glorified.

Now there are many women today who enjoy wearing their capes, sticking out their chests, and declaring to the world how great they are. We've all had our moments where we stood up tall, chest out, red pumps, and cape flapping behind us, like look what I did! However, on the inside, many of us are depleted. We were tired, empty, hungry, fed up, and so much more. What good is it for us to work so hard yet feel so empty inside? We often feel this way because WE try to work things out. WE try to solve all the problems. WE try to be everything to everyone. WE work hard nonstop. The bible tells us in Matthew 13:22 that for those of us who hear the word but care more about the cares of the world and the deceitfulness of riches, you prove to be unfruitful. Ouch.

Ladies, confess with me:

At times I cared more about the cares of the world, being recognized, and about being rich and I didn't realize that I wasn't bearing any internal fruit.

When we have the superwoman complex. we end up with a depleted soul. I mentioned the depleted soul in an earlier chapter. The Superwoman complex will have us thinking, "I can do all things through me" instead of thinking, "I can do all things through Christ." The Superwoman complex will have us juggling our businesses, our families, our social lives, and all the other projects that comes our way. The Superwoman complex will have us BUSY, and you know how much I hate that word because BUSY is in reality counterproductive to a well-balanced life.

The Superwoman complex will have us believing that WE can do anything. The bible reminds us that while things may be lawful it does not mean that we have to do everything. In 1 Corinthians 10:23 (CEB) it says, "Everything is permitted, but everything isn't beneficial. Everything is permitted, but everything doesn't build others up." I talk often about good ideas versus God ideas. That good idea may be good but is it beneficial? Let me share this with you. I spent many days in business accepting good ideas that delayed the God ideas.

I spent many days in business implementing good ideas that delayed God's promises. It was after those good idea moments I realized I was trusting in myself. I was taking matters in my own hands. I was being my own superhero. Your **good** ideas can take you off course but your God ideas can help you stay the course and get you closer to the finish line. You have to make the choice to stop trying to do everything on your own and consult God before you move on.

Sis, it's okay to have good ideas but be encouraged to not act on them immediately. Start writing down some good ideas you've been thinking about lately. Pray over them and let God guide you before making decisions. I know it seems trivial but seek God in every decision you make.

Remember, the superwoman, is not for God's woman. While the superwoman is too busy, God's woman is being still, tuning in to God and digging in His word. The superwoman is not wise for God is the source of all wise instruction. Proverbs 31:26 tells us, "She speaks with wisdom and faithful instruction is on her tongue." God's woman is not trying to be the solution to everyone's problem. She understands that she is to trust in God with all of her heart and lean not on her own understanding (Proverbs 3:5-6)

Superwoman is doing her best to keep up an image while God's woman understands she must fear the Lord and allow Him to order her steps. God is not looking for us to be perfect on the outside. He requires us to give Him some time to help us mature on this journey. Give Him your time, surrender your cape, and cast all of your weariness on Him because He loves you.

Prayer: We thank you Lord for allowing us to seek You. We ask that you strengthen our trust in You as we pray over our ideas, believing that you will bless us to live out Your will for our lives. We ask forgiveness for all of the times we took matters into our own hands and we thank You for providing and carrying us through.

Based on what you read, what truths or promises from God will you affirm over your life? Write your affirmation in the box below.

Affirmation Five: I will slow down and savor quiet moments (Stop rushing my days)

Matthew 6:28 and Psalm 37:7

So ladies, I'll be the first to admit-slowing down was such a struggle for me. I'll just be honest. I enjoy life. I enjoy working. I enjoy socializing. I enjoy spending time with my family. I enjoy helping others. There is absolutely nothing wrong with that. I would pack my calendar up with so many different events, tasks, and reminders so much so that I operated off of two different calendars.

When I started in business, I was BUSY. Stayed up super late. I stayed in the space super late. I took phone calls after 8 PM. I wanted to attend every networking event possible, day and evening. I wanted to host many types of events in the evenings and weekends. In fact, I stayed busy every weekend. This happened week after week and month after month. When I look back over my 2019 calendar, there are only a few weekends when nothing happened for my business but even on those weekends I was doing something.

As I look back over the many times I was constantly on the go I have to confess something, I was not tuned in to God. I wasn't quite hearing His voice at all times. There were moments where I felt like I was in a game of Mario, running over bricks, busting the enemy in the head, punching cactuses, and falling through pipes to get to the next level. During those moments of a rushed life, God was whispering to me, "Slow down my child".

I was taking advice, trying new strategies, and helping people get this and that accomplished. The bible reminds us in Ecclesiastes 9:11 that the race is not given to the fastest one and even the strongest warrior doesn't always win the battle. We have to slow down or we'll miss important marks, lessons, and beautiful moments in life.

Have you ever woke up past your expected time? What makes it worse is if you're not prepared. You find yourself in a state of rush. Clothes thrown everywhere. Heels all over the place. Flat iron in one hand. Make up brush in the other. Toothbrush sticking out your mouth. One pants leg on. You get the picture. Sis, we look a hot mess when we have the morning rush days. Our only focus is to get out the door and on the road to our destination. When I have days of rushing, I forget everything. I'll get to the stop sign and have to turn around to go back home because I forgot my laptop. Get back out the door, let the garage down, and back out the driveway only to back in because I forgot the package I'm supposed to mail off. Here is the problem with rushing. It doesn't make life go faster. In fact, it only makes life messier. When you try to rush life, you miss special and intimate moments with God. On the days when life is chaotic, rushed and frantic, those are the days when I miss important moments with God.

Ladies, confess with me:
Lord forgive us for rushing our days and missing quality moments with you. Help us to humble ourselves before you, giving us time to hear from you and bask in your presence.

Somewhere on this journey called life, we've been bamboozled to think that our busyness and rush of life means that we are doing important things when in fact it is creating an ill society. People have become rude while driving. Stores are filled with express lanes and self-check out. We don't have to cook anymore with Door Dash or with the click of one button we can order our food, walk in the restaurant and pick it up off the shelf without ever having to speak to anyone.

I know as a mom, if I'm not conscious about how I'm spending my time, prayer and devotion just might escape me.

Not good, but we are human. Sometimes we get caught up in the rush of life that we limit our relationship with God to a few minutes here and there just to check it off the to-do list. Done. You and I both know when we put God on the to-do list, life seems to get SUPER crazy and out of whack. When the dust settles, we look at how we have put God on a shelf like a book. The thing I like about our God is that He knows and He will definitely give us a nudge to remind us when we are drifting away.

I'm working on being calendar driven and some days are better than others. What is important is that we carve out **meaningful** time with God. Maybe you don't know where to start and honey that is ok as long as you start or maybe you're like me, always hitting the restart button. The time we spend with God has to be **intentional and consistent** as it helps us draw closer to Him, grow in our faith, and experience everlasting peace and joy in Him.

There are many ways to spend time with Him-prayer, reading His word, singing His praises, joining a women's group or even sharing His goodness with others. I want to encourage you to stay connected to Him. Let's do our part to give God some quality time. If this is an area that's a struggle for you, try these things:

1. Set aside some time each day to read a devotional or simply open the bible and read it. There are a million devotionals online and in print that are connected to God's word and His principles for life. Get a devotional or a bible reading guide that focuses on areas you want to improve like faith or prayer.
2. Spend the first 5 minutes of your day in prayer and giving thanks to God for His many blessings. What a great way to get your day going. But… if the first 5 minutes does not work for you (not a morning person like me), be sure to carve out some quiet time throughout the day-on your lunch break, when the kiddos are napping, or when the household is sleeping. You get it. Carving out time helps you to be accountable and intentional with our time. You will find that those quiet moments will turn into everlasting moments with God.
3. Share your faith and testimonies of your experiences with others. Not only will you inspire someone else but also you will be reminded of just how good God is to you. You can do this by joining a group online or in your church or posting your blessings instead of your messiness. Doing so

is a great way to stay connected to the Master and a way to get people connected to Him.

Prayer: Lord we've spent so much time rushing life, doing life, and being all to everyone. We know that only through you can we live, move and have our being. Putting you first only gives us the fuel we need to make it through our day. Help us to stay connected to you. Continue nudging us when we are steering down the wrong path. We're grateful for your love and the time you bless us with each day.

Based on what you read, what truths or promises from God will you affirm over your life? Write your affirmation in the box below.

While the superwoman is too busy, God's woman is being still, tuning in to God and digging in His word.

Affirmation: Six: I will rest because it is requirement (God says to rest)

Genesis 2:3

Have you looked at your calendar lately? Yes, your calendar. Well depending when you are affirming your life, it may look pretty empty. At this moment, as I'm writing this, the world is in the midst of a pandemic. Life has come to a screeching halt. Businesses are closed. Schools are closed. Anything deemed non-essential has stopped.

I didn't foresee any of this. I talked about the sickness briefly when it first appeared but that was it. Let me shift back to October of 2019 when I first started writing this book. I had a speaking engagement and started writing about the busy woman and when writing my notes, God stopped me. For weeks, I could not focus on what to say and finally, the night before the event, everything He wanted me to share, He downloaded. As I was writing my session, He brought back to remembrance every area of my life where He was working on my behalf even in my busy seasons. Let me say that again, even in my busy season, God still kept me.

Here is some of what God said to me on October 10, 2018, to share with the women:

James 4:7-10 (MSG), "So let God work His will in you. Yell a loud No to the devil. And watch him scamper Say a quiet yes to God and he'll be there in no time. Stop dabbling in sin. Quit playing the field." We can't be on fire for God today and falling out tomorrow crying over every situation. Give it God. God calls us for purpose and when we play the field and not give our yes to God, He'll give that purpose over to someone else. Now is not the time to get busy. Now is the time to chase God down like you've never chased Him before. Don't allow satan to get in your membrane and tell you that you can't do it. Yes you can and you do have time. God gives us time. You have to use it wisely. Plan. It's the only way. I charge you to Pray, plan and pursue. God has something for you. If your plate is full, you will miss it.

Plan out your days. Plan your family time. Plan your family days. Find your days to bask in the Word of God. When God is constantly waking you up at a certain time, God is wanting to hear from you and wanting you to hear from Him. He has a purpose for you. Some of us need to get off of Facebook and stop watching Netflix and get in God and we need to do it NOW.

Ladies, confess with me:

Lord I confess that there are times when I'm in a state of busyness. My days are off, I'm tired and don't seek you. Help me to find rest in you when I'm weary and rest when I'm just plain old worn out.

I share a portion of my message because there are times when God calls you to rest, where you cut everything and everyone off for a time so He can have your undivided attention. Before I wrote the above message, I had just come off a period of rest-resting in Christ and physical rest.

I was working super hard at so many things, mentally, emotionally, and physically I was drained. I became ill and the Lord said for me to rest. During that period of time, I begin seeking to understand. I turned everything off- facebook, facebook messenger, no response to emails, silenced my phone. All so that I could tune in to what God was saying.

As I sat still, God showed me areas where I wasn't trusting Him fully. Jesus reminds us in His word to lay our burdens on Him and He will give us rest (Matthew 11:28-30) So many of us can't rest because we are too busy-busy carrying weights that we have no business carrying; busy solving problems that we have no business trying to solve.

Do me a favor. Go outside and look around at the beauty of nature, look at yourself in the mirror, and find joy in what took six days to create. I mean God deserved a day to REST. Now sit back and think about all the work you do-the respective roles you play in life, the business you've built, the career position you hold, the friends you connect with- all of this requires you to REST sis. Your physical body requires a day of rest. Don't get caught up in this hustling hype, where people are telling you that real entrepreneurs, real teachers, and real leaders don't sleep but work hard and burn the midnight oil. LIES! We are created in the image and likeness of God and if He rested from physical labor so should we. What if we worked like God and rested like Him? I truly believed that if we abide in His work ethic, some of us would be much better. Rest is the reset our bodies need in order to make it through the week. After all, think about all the events that happened after God rested.

We can only fulfill our God assignments when we get rid of busy and chase God down. He is wanting more of us. He is calling for us to go deeper in him. We have to move beyond these five minute prayers with God and these 3 day devotions with God and dig in the word. The things that you've been asking, the desires of your heart, they don't come through Facebook fasts. They don't come through TV fasts. And sis, listen, there is nothing wrong with fasting from social media and doing other fasts from things like sweets, etc. But a surefire way to subject your flesh is to turn down a meal or two or three. Remember, these things come through fasting and praying. In Deuteronomy He commands us to love the lord with all of our HEARTS! When we obey our God, when we chase him down, He said that he will set us HIGH and all these blessings will come upon you and overtake you.

Prayer: Lord, you have blessed each of us with the same measurable amount of time. Help us to slow down and give our minds and body the rest it needs to use our time wisely. Rest is commandment from you so that we can fulfill our calling from you.

Based on what you read, what truths or promises from God will you affirm over your life? Write your affirmation in the box below.

Affirmation Seven: I will trust in Christ because He is my strength.

Isaiah 40:31

We are creatures of habit, often looking back over the years at our losses and gains. How we let go of friendships, but gained a closer circle. How we let go of bad relationships, but found a closeness with ourselves. How we lost a battle, but renewed our strength. I too find myself looking back at some losses but counting my blessings as I move forward. Life is a continuous journey of learning and growing. Without this process, we would be like the tree planted but not bearing any fruit.

I remember we went on a family vacation to the beach and can I be honest? I didn't think about anything related to work, business, podcasts, social media posts, products, services, etc. NOTHING! Sometimes you just have to turn it all off. The weather forecast called for heavy rain and thunder on our way home but I thought we left the bad weather at the beach. When I hit the interstate, I could see the storm ahead and it didn't look anything pretty. I began to slow down and just pray. It was the only thing I wanted to do at that moment. It was that bad. The wind was howling and the trees were bowing to the ground. The rain poured so hard I was unable to see. Cars were passing me full speed ahead but I drove at a steady pace and I just kept whispering Jesus's name.

During the storm, I didn't rely on the car, the headlights, nor my husband. I only relied on Christ. What felt like an hour actually lasted 10 minutes. As I drove out of the storm, the sun broke through the clouds and as I looked ahead, it looked as if the interstate didn't even encounter a storm. I looked back in my rear view mirror, and I could see the storm behind me. One by one cars came out of the storm behind me unharmed. The roads were clear. No water. No debris. I made it through the storm.

Here is a reality: there are times we look back and we become disappointed. We question why things happened a certain way. We don't feel well about our decisions. We may feel ashamed. We didn't forgive. We didn't forget. Sis, please know that's a trick of the enemy. He creates this trap to keep us bound in our hearts, our thoughts, and in our past.

Ladies, confess with me:

Lord, there are times we look back and we have doubts, fears, anxiety, or other emotions that rob us of our joy that you've promised. We need your help.

The Lord reminded me that my storms are just like the one I described. Remember after Jesus was teaching the large crowd, He wanted to rest (see even Jesus rested). He and the apostles decided to take a boat to another town where the crowds were not so large. While Jesus was asleep, a storm was brewing on the ocean with heavy winds and waves that terrified the apostles. They awoke Him about the storm and all Jesus said was be still. The winds and the waves ceased. Jesus was with them the entire time, eventhough He was resting. He rebuked them because they didn't have faith or trust that while He was there, the apostles would be fine.

On this journey called life, there will be some days we may or may not see the storms coming ahead. We must trust God at all times no matter the situation. No matter how hard the wind blows. No matter what other people are doing in their lives to pass you by. No matter if there are times we cannot see what lies ahead. If we keep our minds on Jesus, like it says in the scripture, He will give us peace. Have you ever seen someone who was in a fight? Their hair is a mess, clothes all tattered, and they are out of breath. A hot mess I'll say. Job 23:10 says, "He knows the way I take and when He has tried me, I will come out as pure gold." Trust and believe, when the storm is over, it won't even look like we've been through a storm because God is our strength. We have to tune our ears, eyes and heart to His words and His promises. That's where we find our strength! I learned a long time ago that I can make all the plans I want to but it is Christ who directs my path (Proverbs 16:9).

I looked back in my rear view mirror after that storm, and I believe God was reminding me of what He brought me through. I didn't look back like Lot's wife, with a desire to return in my heart, for I had no desire to turn around but it definitely was a reminder that God keeps His promises:

- He will never leave you nor forsake you (Deuteronomy 31:6)
- He delivers us from our afflictions (Psalm 34:17-20)
- He supplies all of our needs (Philippians 4:19)

It's ok to look back at the storms God delivered you from so that you can praise Him and be prepared for the future storms He'll carry you through. The old song says "count your blessings, name them one by one. Count your many blessings to see what God has done!"

Recently a friend of mine started a bathroom renovation project. She showed us pictures of the bathroom before, during and after. On the first day of renovation, she knew that things would look a little messy but when she sent the picture to her girls, they were expecting something different. Every day she checked on the progress. Some days it looked fine and others it looked messy, but there was some progress.

I am not sure who told me that taking on your dreams would be easy. That I would not be exhausted some days. That my patience would fluctuate. That my confidence would be tested. When chasing your dreams-an idea, a book deal, a business venture, or a new career-you can organize your days, take a thousand courses, or meet with expert after expert, but in order to succeed, you have to understand that your ability to bounce back will help you in the long run.

On this journey, we will all encounter storms. Life will get messy. Days won't be easy. Call His name. Stick close to Him. Praise Him. He will deliver you!

Prayer: Lord we thank you that the storms we experience you will not let them overtake us. We thank you for being with us in the midst of our storms. We ask that you forgive us times when we didn't lean on your strength to make it through but we praise you for being with us through it all.

Based on what you read, what truths or promises from God will you affirm over your life? Write your affirmation in the box below.

Affirmation Eight: I will enjoy every moment of peace because God is my priority.

Psalm 118:24

"So what's one of your greatest assets," he asked during my interview. I said boldly, "I'm great at multitasking." He laughed and my boldness coupled with a confident smile suddenly turned into a confused yet defeated look. His words, "For it is impossible for man to skillfully complete several tasks at once without one or more of those tasks being fulfilled to the best of your ability. Therefore, young lady, I would prefer, because of the nature of this job, to have a candidate who can organize and prioritize his/her task so that each task receives the attention it deserves." After a few minutes of discussion, he told me to avoid using that term because leaders want employees who can prioritize not multitask.

Maybe you are the person who likes to take care of several tasks all at once, but if you truly think about it, that is super overwhelming and difficult for the brain to process. Balance says you give equal time and attention to the different areas of your life whether it is work, church, family, marriage, friendships but here is the kicker for me-balance is not realistic. When my priority list is out of order, meaning when I put something or someone over the important things in my life, well guess what-my life gets crazy.

So here is my priority-God.Family.Work (friends are included with family). In James chapter 4 it tells us to draw close to God and He will draw close to us. Additionally, there are several verses in the New Testament that talk to us about the headship and Christ being first. If we put God first, everything else will fall into place, but the moment we put our jobs first, our families first, our desires and wants first, things seem to get a bit whacky. Think about the days we don't spend time with God. We feel rushed, overwhelmed, weary, tired and sometimes defeated.

Ladies, confess with me:
Lord, we don't always prioritize what's important in life.
We honor you for giving us time and ask that you help us to put you first in all we do.

My main focus is to be diligent in all that I do. One area I want to be diligent in is seeking God with my whole heart. It's a priority. The word of God tells us to "seek ye first the kingdom of God and all of His right ways of living." In the Bible, we learn about God's love for Israel over and over in the various scriptures, even telling them He loved them with an everlasting love. Wow! He wanted one main thing from them and that was to love Him with their wholeheart. He wanted them to turn from their wicked ways, their complaining ways, their idol worshipping, and anything that distracted them from receiving His everlasting love.

In Amos 3, we learn about God's relationship with Israel. Israel was the only people God had such an intimate relationship with. He made it very clear that because of their ways, He was angry. Israel wasn't faithful consistently. Look, I don't want to chase goals first. I no longer want to chase status or material possessions. I want to seek God. By putting God first, I know that all other areas of my life will fall into place. Being diligent in seeking Him, helps you give your best yes! When we are diligent in seeking God, "…all these things will be added unto us" according to the word of God. Blessings don't always have to be tangible things but any reward from God is worth having for in the word it says that "He rewards those who diligently seek Him."

Sometimes we get distracted by our surroundings-family, social life, social media, or television- and we find ourselves off track. It happens because none of us are perfect. However, if we find ourselves getting off track, seek God. If we find ourselves becoming weary, seek God. We have to be careful because distractions are dangerous. Distractions can rob you of your time, your energy, and your priorities and most importantly, it shows our God that we are not faithful to Him.

In this life, we have to do as the director who interviewed me said-prioritize. If you have stuff on your plate that is causing your life to be unbalanced, it's time to remove it. If you are not putting God first, it is time to think about the hierarchy that rules your life. If that hierarchy is out of order, life is unbalanced. If you are giving too much time to something (TV can be my too much time) and not enough time to do other things that are important in your life, it is time to disconnect. When life is balanced and in order we have peace. Isaiah 26:3 says, "He will keep us in perfect peace if we keep our minds stayed on Him."

Don't you want that peace to linger in your relationships and clothe you with love, strength and joy as you go through your days? Well here is your answer: stop trying to multitask your way through life and remember priorities and order brings us into alignment with God. When we have peace, we have joy that the world did not give us and it surely cannot take it away.

Take an honest look at yourself and think about what you need to get rid of in order to make God a priority. Carrying bad habits creates unnecessary weights that can ultimately kill us on our journey. When we continue to hold on people, habits, and circumstances, slowly but surely the light at the end of the tunnel will become dim.

I've worked diligently to apply these four strategies in order to make God a priority so that I can experience peace. I'm sharing these with you too:

1. **The Need to Please–** We've all been bitten by this bug and for some people this is not an issue. BUT for those of us that have the bite mark still on us I want to encourage you to quit worrying about what others think. Quit trying to appease to others. What others think and want from you does not matter in terms of success. Now don't get me wrong, you have people in your tribe who want the best for you. They matter. But for the naysayers, the questioners, the people who feel they have all the answers. Bye Bye! You have to determine within yourself that no matter where you are on your journey, other people cannot and will not determine your level of joy and peace.

2. **Stop Procrastination**– Raise your hand if you struggle with this! Burning the midnight oil produces my best work. For real ladies, it does. But in reality the procrastination bug creates a sense of unnecessary rush and it takes away from my ability to rest. What I also learned is that procrastination has something to do with how I view myself and my ability to complete something. It hits that area we call confidence. When I procrastinate, my mind starts racing with all the words, work, thoughts, and ideas trying to put pieces together as I get closer to the deadline. When you have a deadline to complete a task, allow yourself some time daily to work towards the deadline. You'll walk away feeling more **confident** and accomplished in your work. Can we say peace as well?

3. **Delaying Actions**– The bible tells us to write the vision. So many times we have written out our vision, given it to God and yet, we are afraid to move forward with our actions. This fear comes because we want to know the outcome or we are again, worried about what others think. In all times of our lives, whether it's the beginning of a year or

middle of the year, God wants to put our faith to work. Pray away that fear and put your trust in Him. There is no way for us to know the outcome for everything unless He shows us. Your faith will become stronger if you only trust Him. Your vision will come pass if you only trust Him. The best thing you can do right now is take your leap of faith (and as I'm typing this, I'm speaking to myself) and start working. When God gives you the vision, put your faith to work and watch God work!

4. **Taking on Too Much**– I have to keep talking about this because I hear people say how tired they are or how much they are overwhelmed. This is a lesson you don't want to have to learn over and over like me. I want to encourage you to stop doing the work for people, stop over committing yourself, and stop saying yes to things that may take you away from your God-given tasks, tasks that will bring Him glory as you live out your purpose. For example, I had to press pause on some tasks years ago at church. But it's the work of the Lord, Tamika. You're right. However, my first ministry is at home and when things became overwhelming in all that I was doing in church ministry, home became a

second priority and that is not how God calls us to lead as mothers and wives. Take heed to the voice of God and allow Him to direct your path so that you know where your "Yes Lord" answers need to go. For some it may be comforting a friend in need. For others it may be turning down a girls night out to minister to the homeless. You may be a wife, daughter, leader, church facilitator or whatever. When God can get the glory out of all we do, we are giving our best Yes.

There are times where we may fall off the wagon a bit or even a few times due to busyness, family changes, work changes but always find ways to bounce back. Your ability to bounce back is a testimony for your comeback! When you bounceback, you can stand up and rest in God's peace.

Prayer: Lord, we let the weights of life and ways of life burden us at time. We procrastinate. We say yes. We over commit. We don't prioritize. Help us to better steward the precious time you've given us so that we can experience your peace.

Based on what you read, what truths or promises from God will you affirm over your life? Write your affirmation in the box below.

About the Author

Tamika S. Washington is a work-from-home mom who started her journey of entrepreneurship with podcasting and blogging and needing a community to connect and collaborate with other like-minded individuals. She needed a space to work outside of the home while feeding the need for a productive, collaborative environment to grow personally and professionally. After starting her blog and podcast, and taking a leap of faith, she and her husband created ConverSpace. Tamika's background is in education coaching, professional development, and content and technical writing. She is a native of Columbia, South Carolina, and is married to Devin Washington. They are the proud parents of Little Miss Faith Bellamy. As mompreneur, Tamika's motto is to live on purpose, love her kingdom assignment, and learn daily. She creates collaborative events and opportunities for busy women and start ups to grow personally and professionally.

Tamika is available for speaking engagements including keynotes, workshop facilitating, and panel opportunities. Visit www.iamtamikal.com to for booking information, to shop and learn about upcoming events.

Follow Tamika on Social Media

www.instagram.com/iamtamikal

www.twitter.com/iamtamikal

www.ingramcontent.com/pod-product-compliance
Lightning Source LLC
Chambersburg PA
CBHW071230160426
43196CB00012B/2461